HOW TO DRAW
——— ANIMALS ———
for Kids!

EMAIL US AT

modernkidpress@gmail.com

TO GET FREE GOODIES!

Just title the email "Animal Freebies!"
And we will send some extra
surprises your way!

Find more books from Modern Kid Press on Amazon!

This book belongs to:

_____

_____

_____

Let's learn to draw!

Learning to draw is easy with the grid copy method! The grid method has been used for centuries and is a wonderful way to work on your observation and proportion skills while drawing!

To get started, grab a pencil and a good eraser. Even the best artists have to erase!

TIPS FOR DRAWING:

- Always start in pencil and use light strokes. You can always go back and erase or darken your strokes!
- Take your time! Slow down and really focus on what you are drawing.
- Sketch an outline first then go back and add detail, darken your strokes, and add color!
- Practice, practice, practice! Drawing is a skill that takes time to master!

THE GRID COPY METHOD:

The grid copy method breaks down each full image into smaller boxes allowing you to focus on and simply draw one box of the picture at a time. Start with grid box A1 and work your way down to box F7.

When you are drawing, focus only on what is in that particular box that you are working on. Try to draw exactly what you see in the box!

Start here!

Focus on one box at a time!

When you're finished, add your own details or color your masterpiece!

Fox

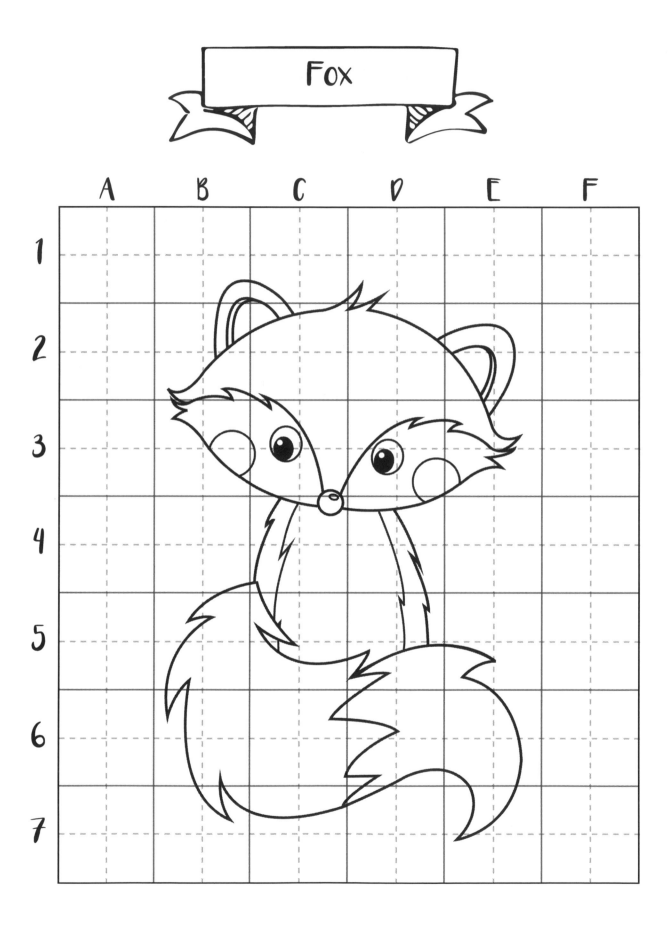

your turn!

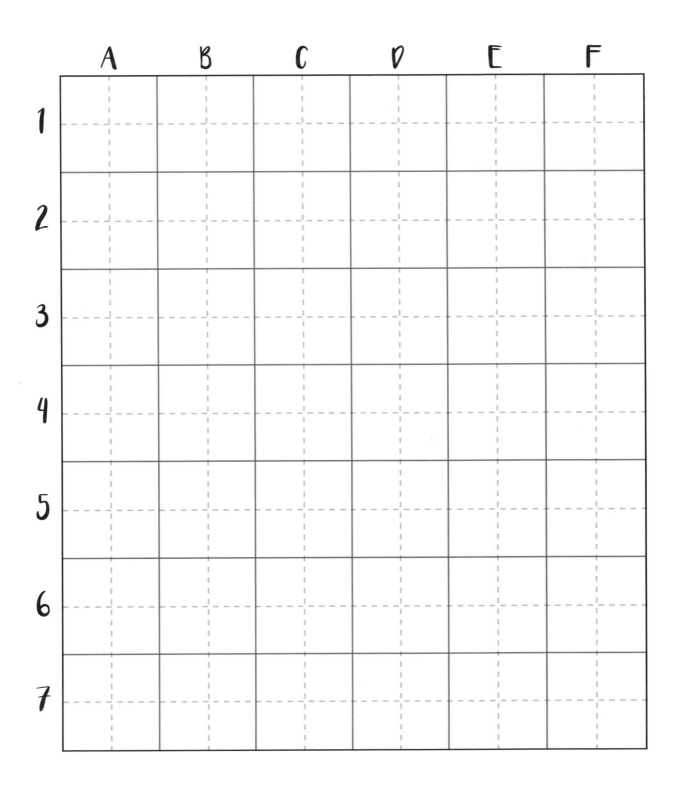

Trace it!

Try it on your own!

Owl

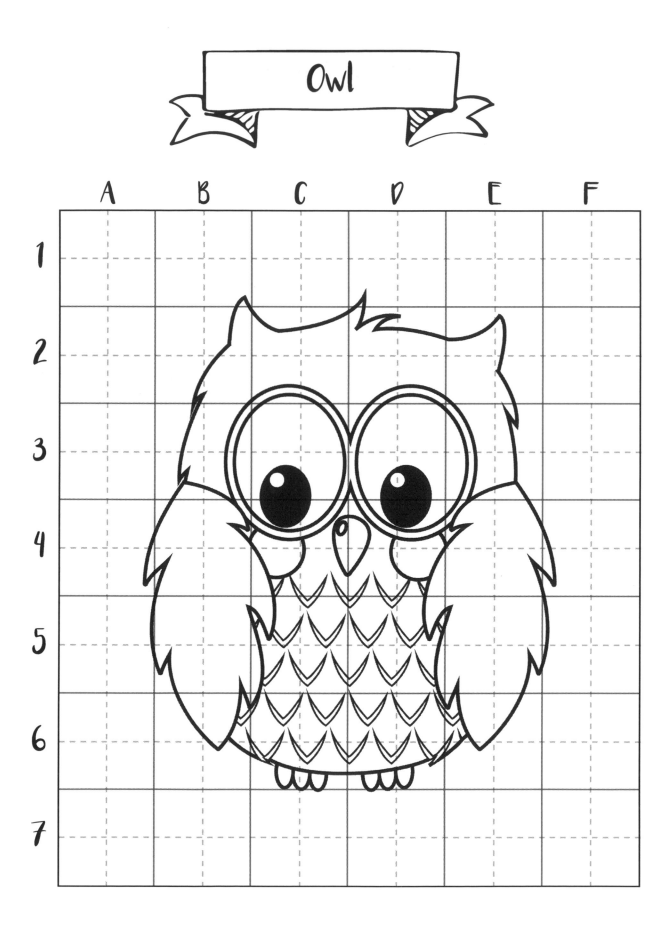

	A	B	C	D	E	F
1						
2						
3						
4						
5						
6						
7						

your turn!

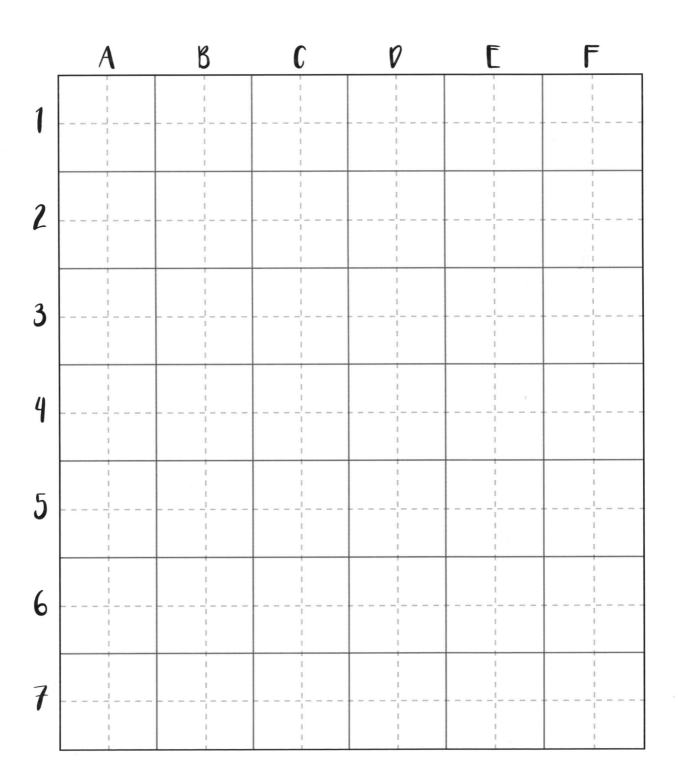

Trace it!

Try it on your own!

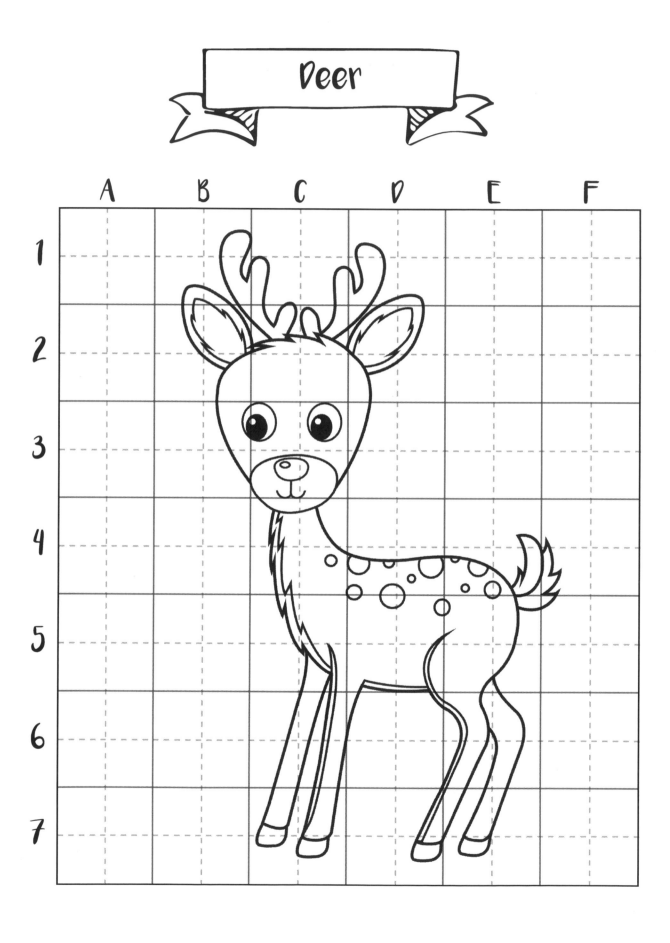

Deer

Your turn!

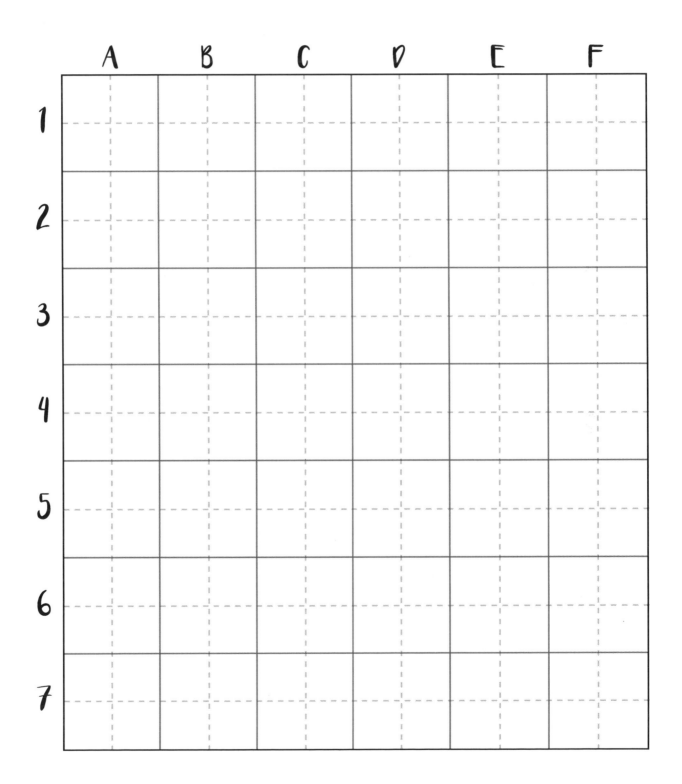

Trace it!

Try it on your own!

Butterfly

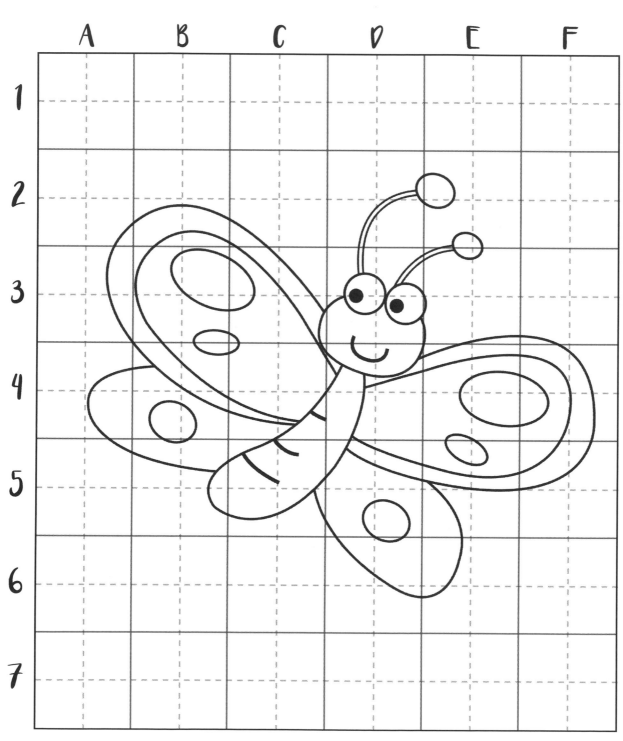

	A	B	C	D	E	F
1						
2						
3						
4						
5						
6						
7						

Your turn!

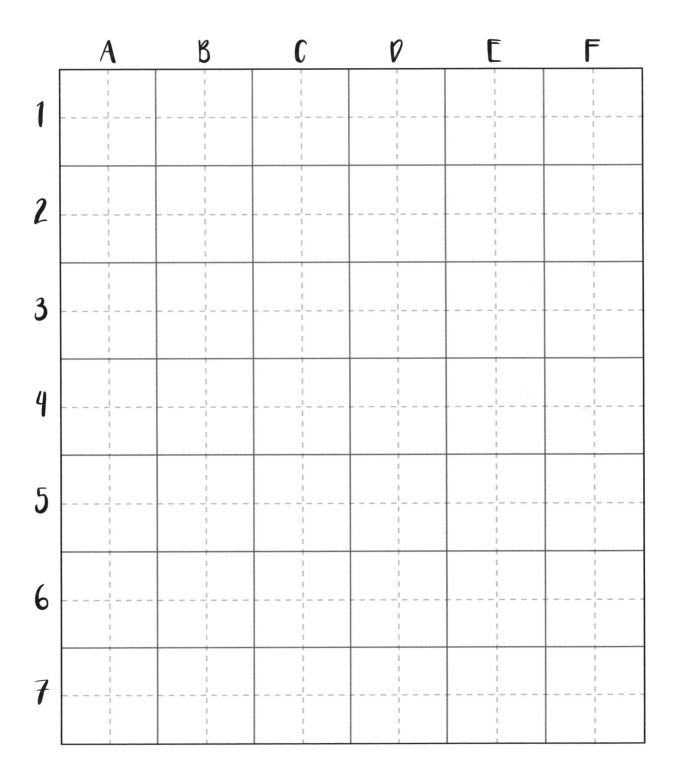

Trace it!

Try it on your own!

Elephant

your turn!

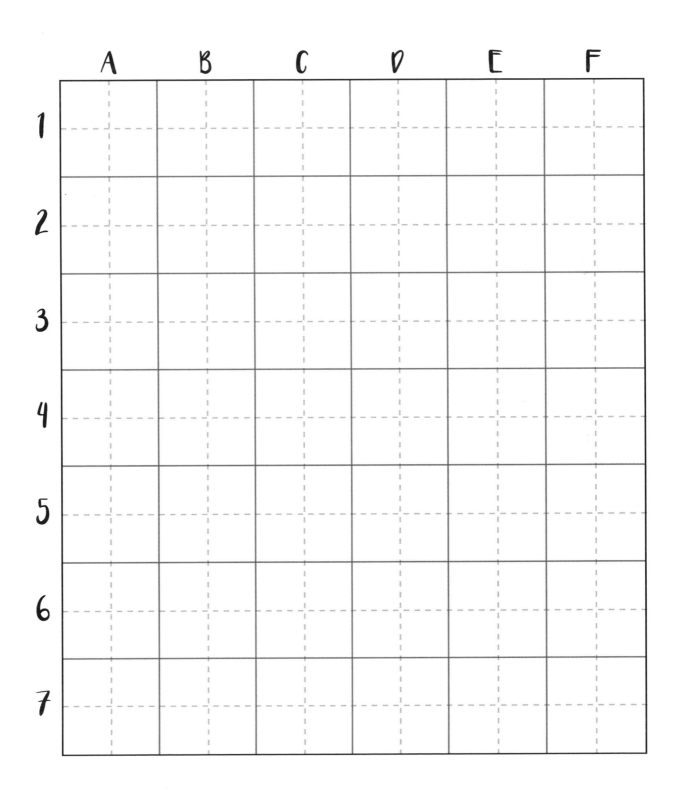

Trace it!

Try it on your own!

Giraffe

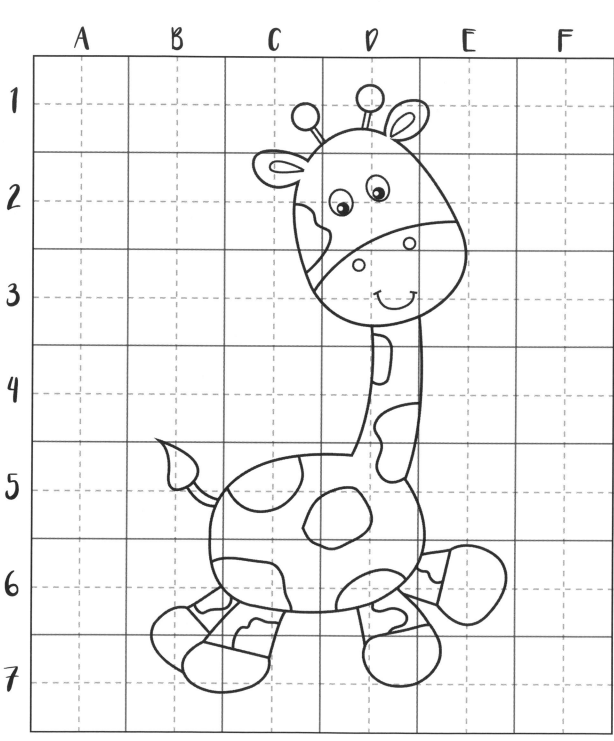

Your turn!

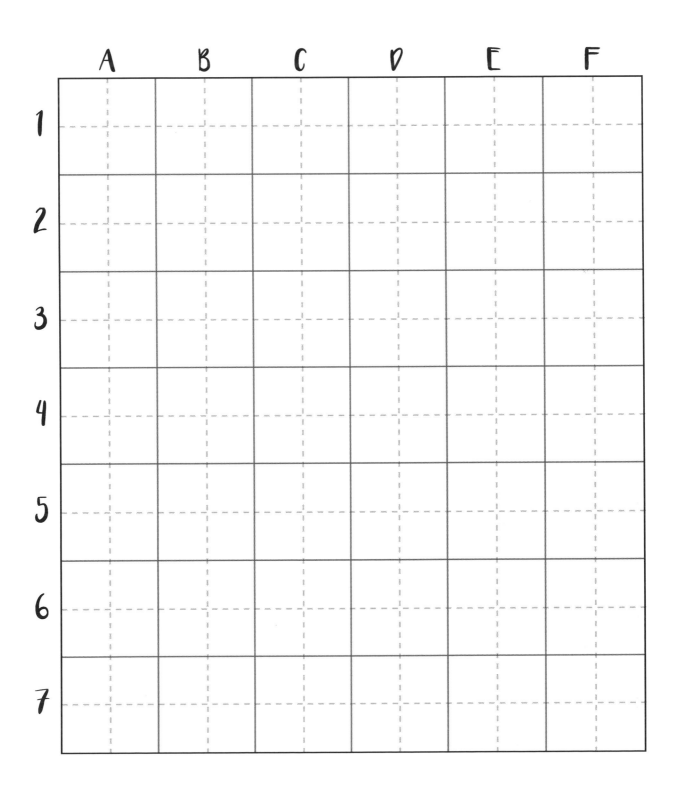

Trace it!

Try it on your own!

Hedgehog

	A	B	C	D	E	F
1						
2						
3						
4						
5						
6						
7						

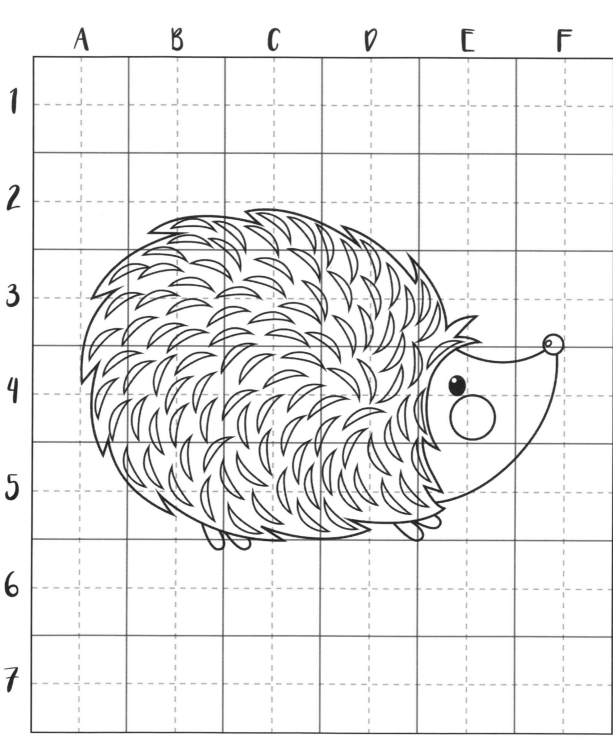

Your turn!

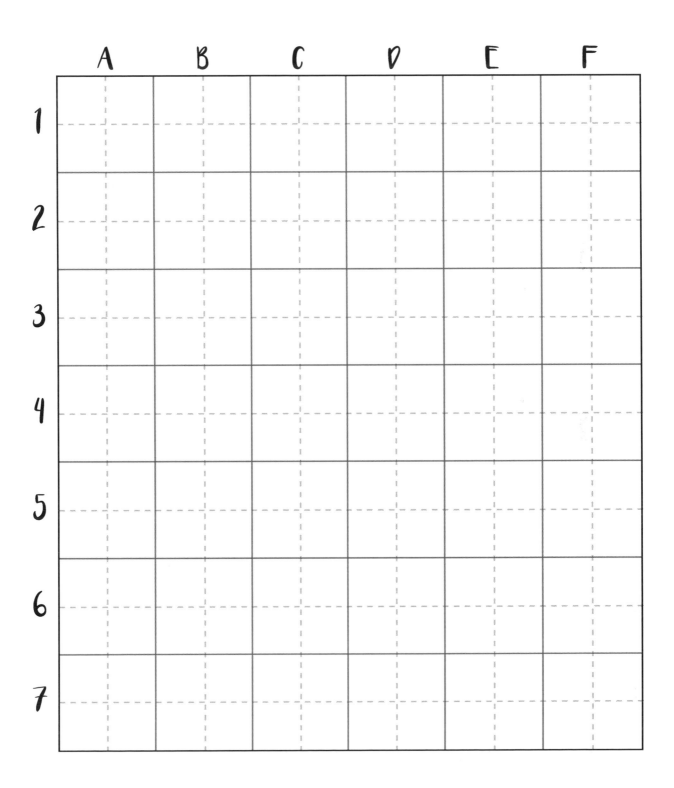

Trace it!

Try it on your own!

Ladybug

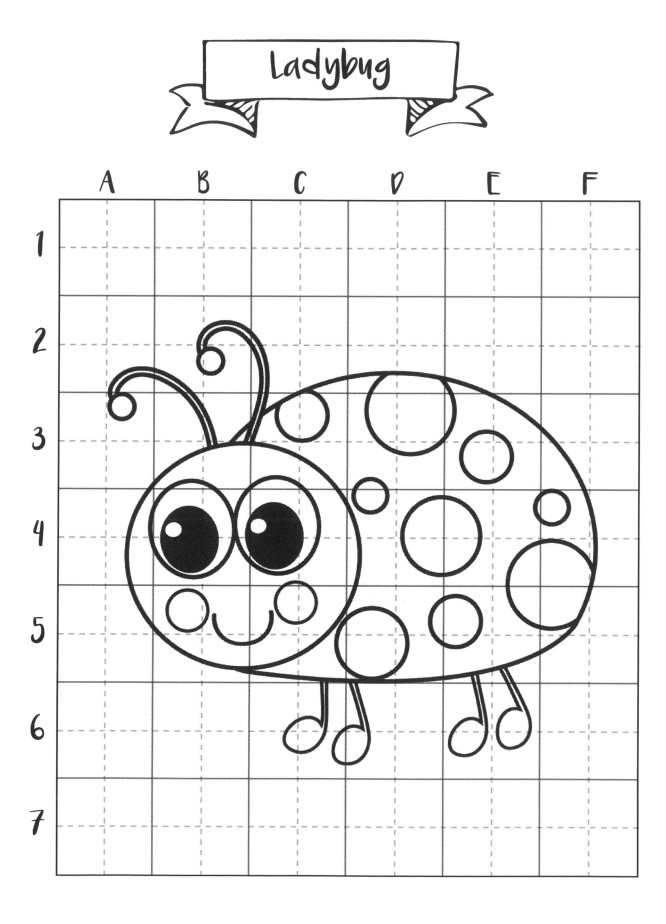

your turn!

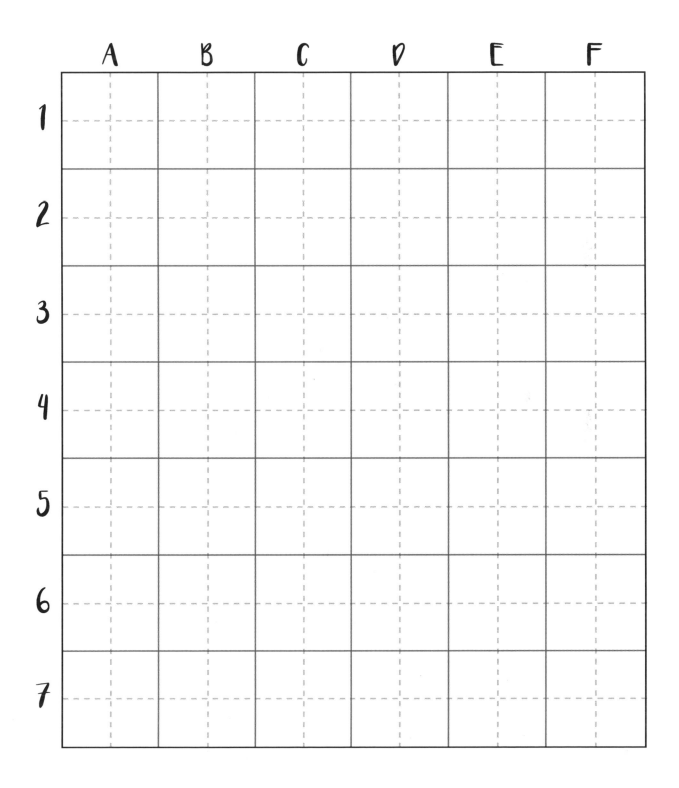

Trace it!

Try it on your own!

Bunny

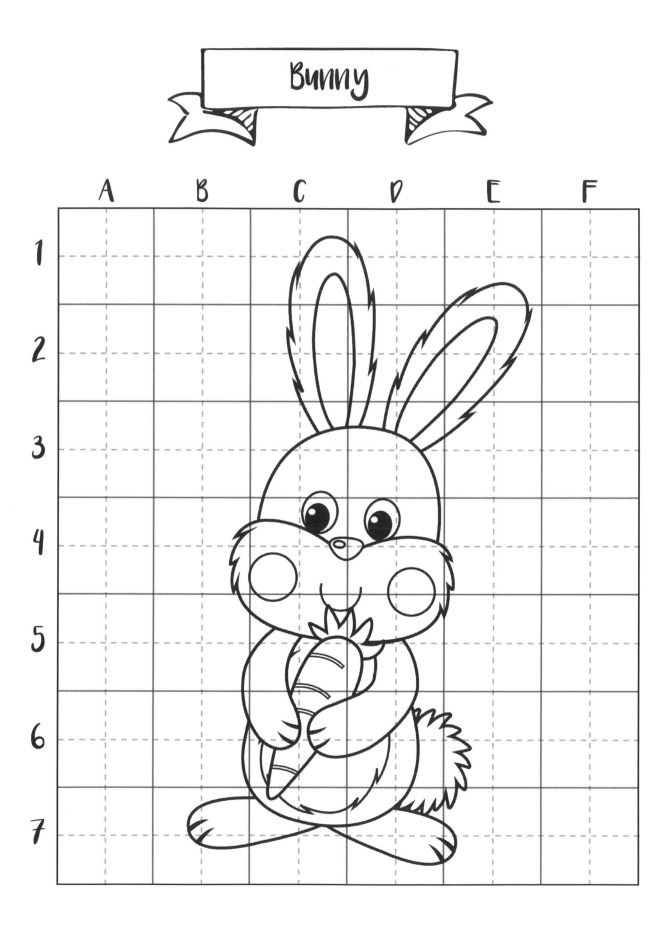

	A	B	C	D	E	F
1						
2						
3						
4						
5						
6						
7						

Your turn!

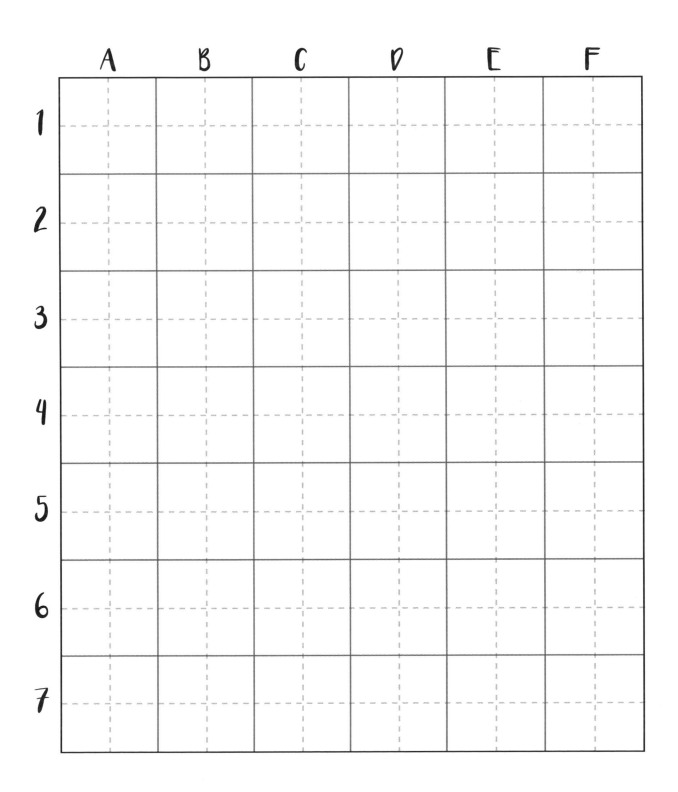

Trace it!

Try it on your own!

Frog

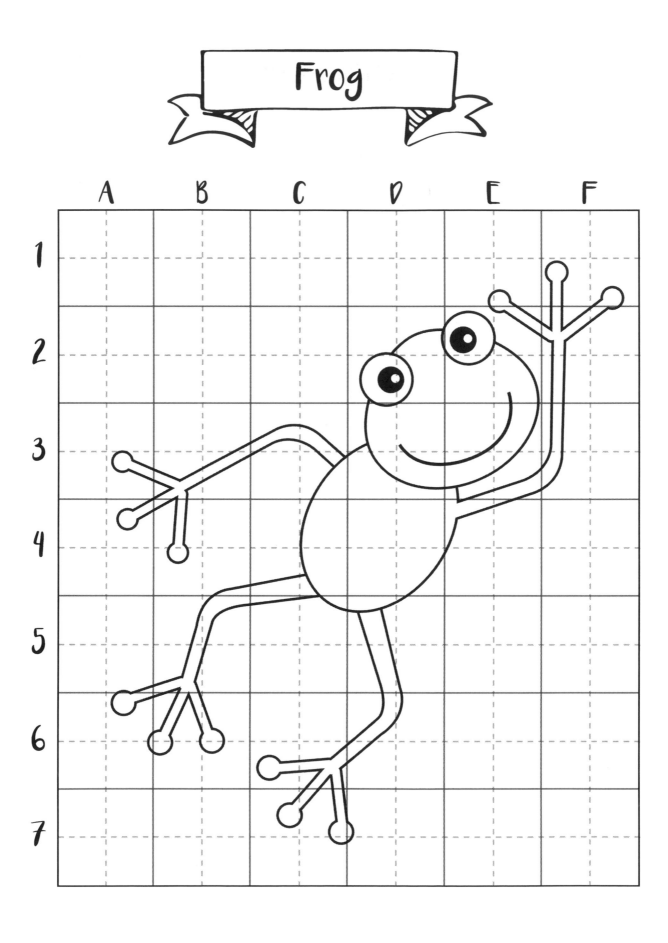

	A	B	C	D	E	F
1						
2						
3						
4						
5						
6						
7						

your turn!

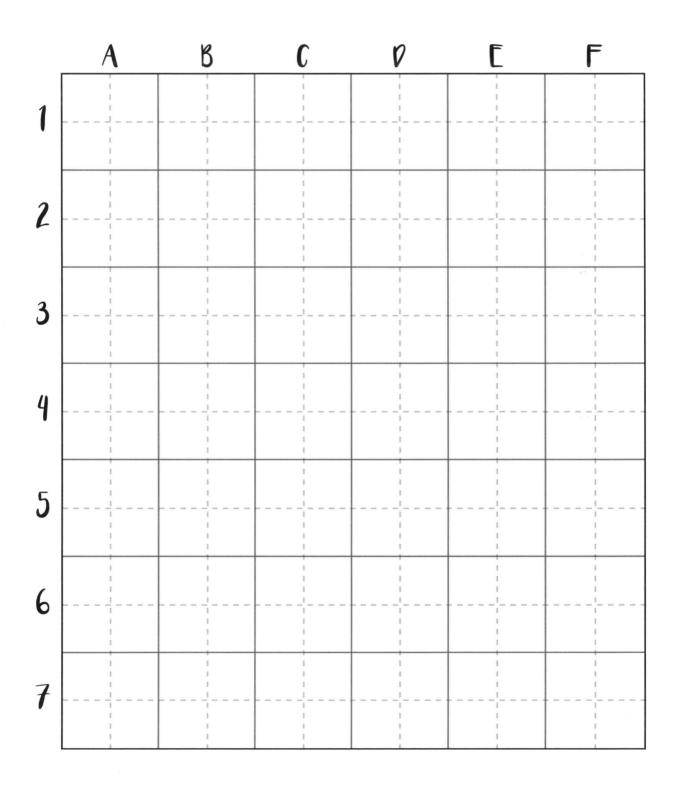

Trace it!

Try it on your own!

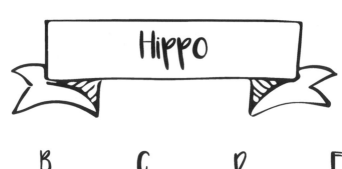

Hippo

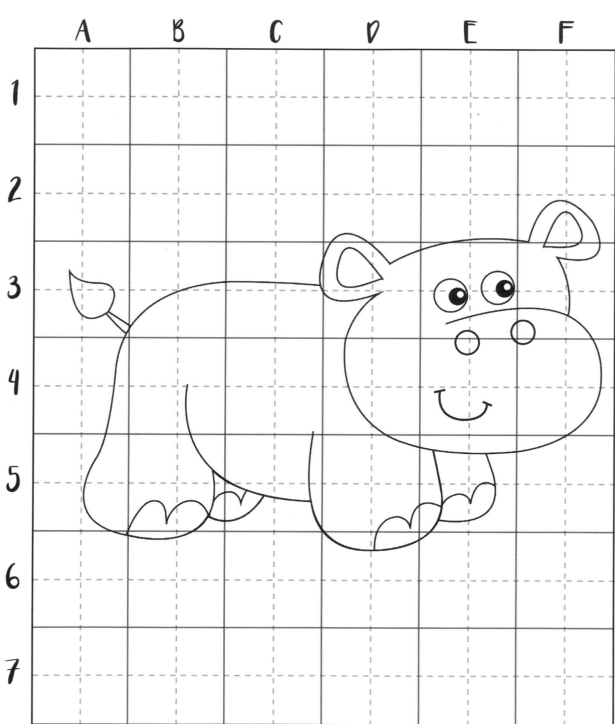

A   B   C   D   E   F

1

2

3

4

5

6

7

Your turn!

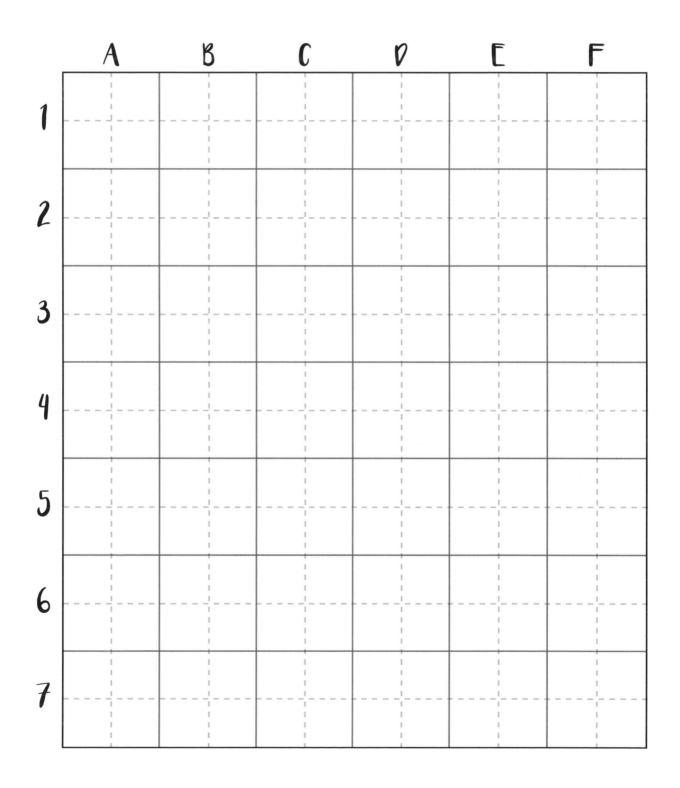

Trace it!

Try it on your own!

Lion

	A	B	C	D	E	F
1						
2						
3						
4						
5						
6						
7						

Your turn!

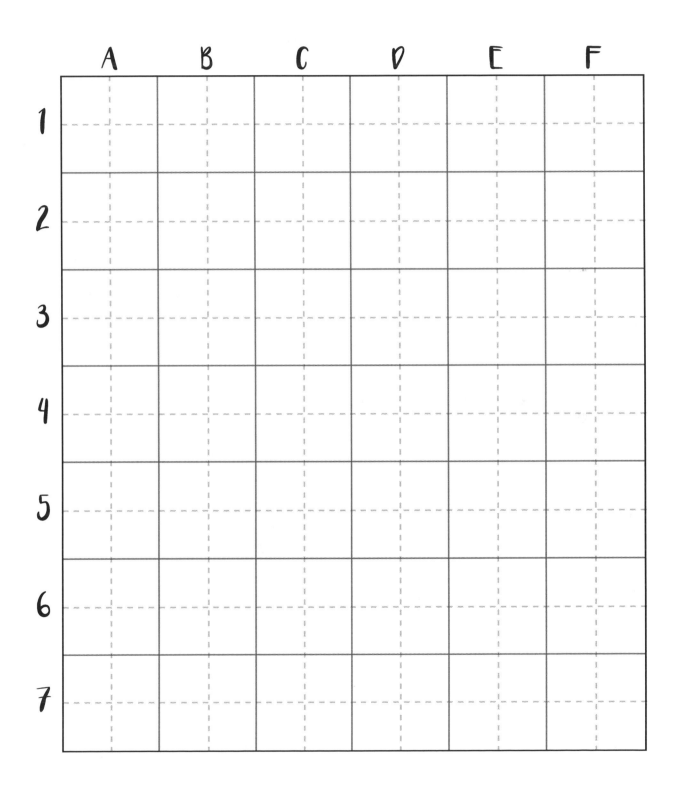

Trace it!

Try it on your own!

Raccoon

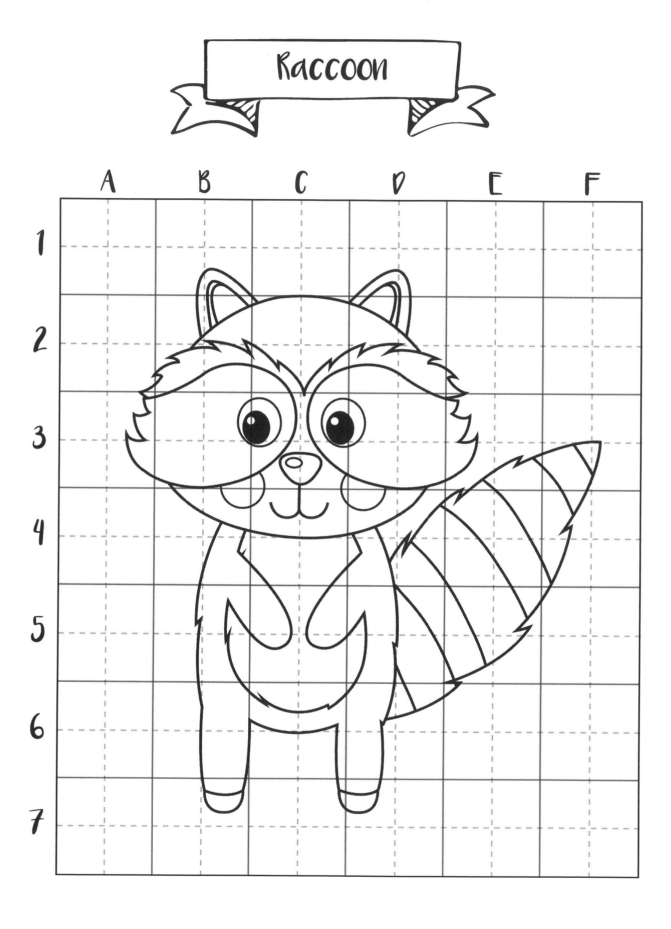

Your turn!

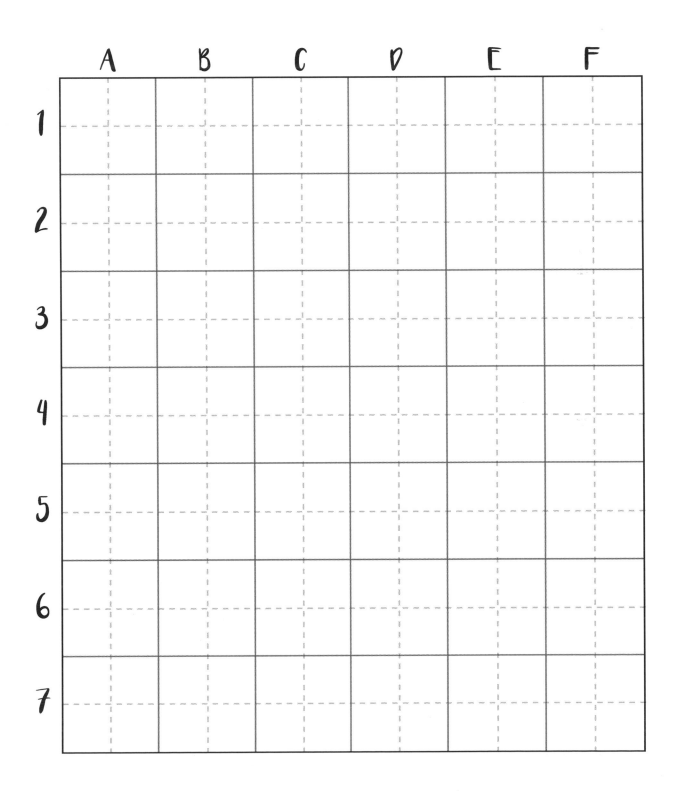

Trace it!

Try it on your own!

Snail

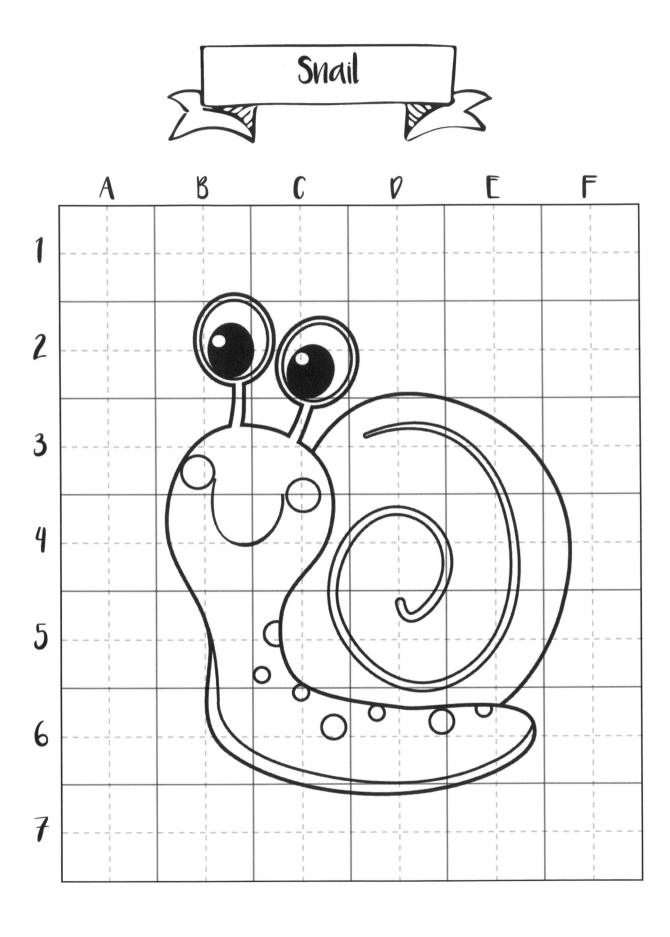

	A	B	C	D	E	F
1						
2						
3						
4						
5						
6						
7						

Your turn!

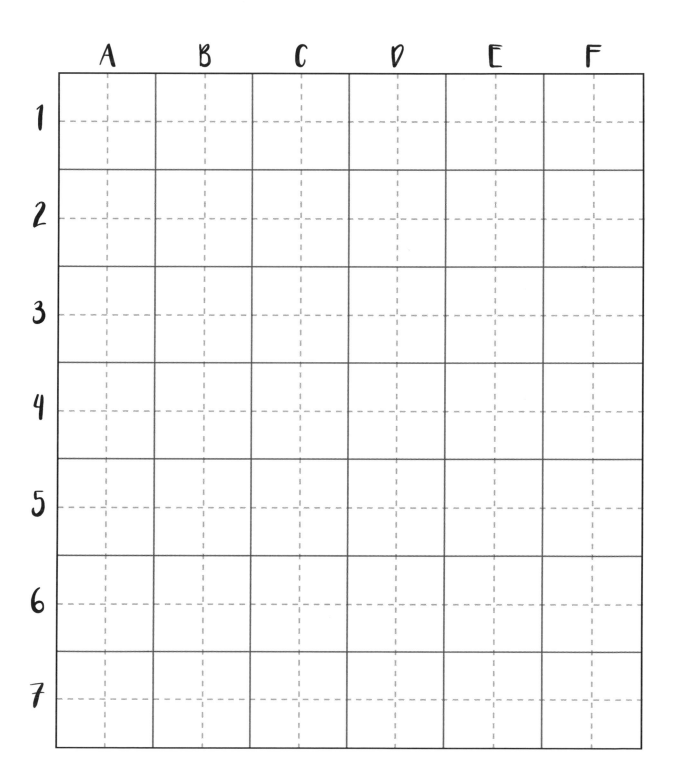

Trace it!

Try it on your own!

Squirrel

Your turn!

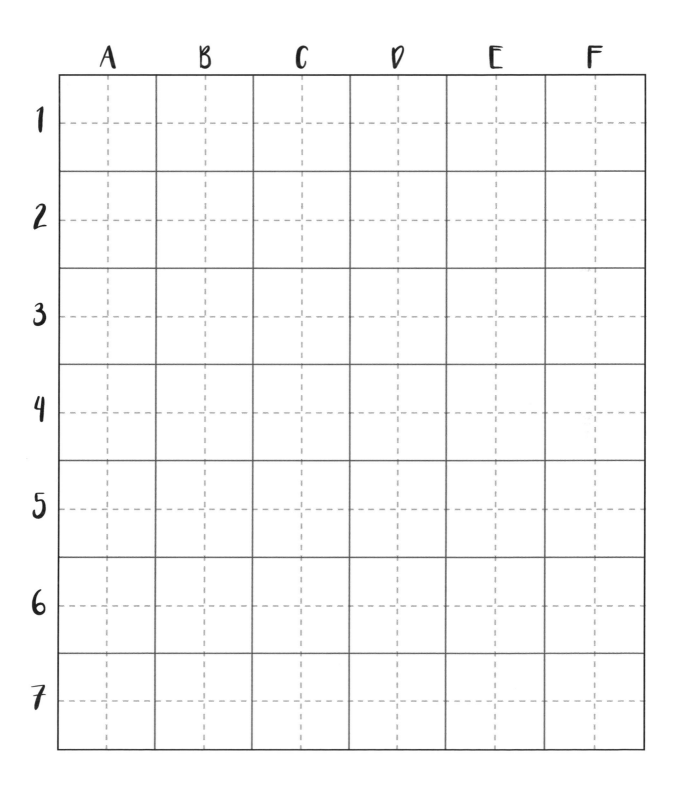

Trace it!

 Try it on your own!

Monkey

	A	B	C	D	E	F
1						
2						
3						
4						
5						
6						
7						

Your turn!

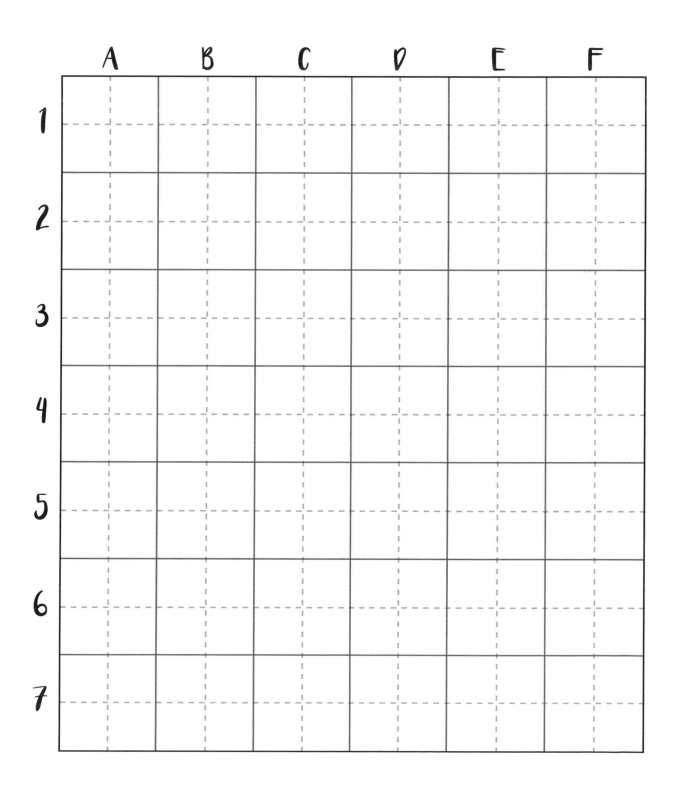

Trace it!

Try it on your own!

Parrot

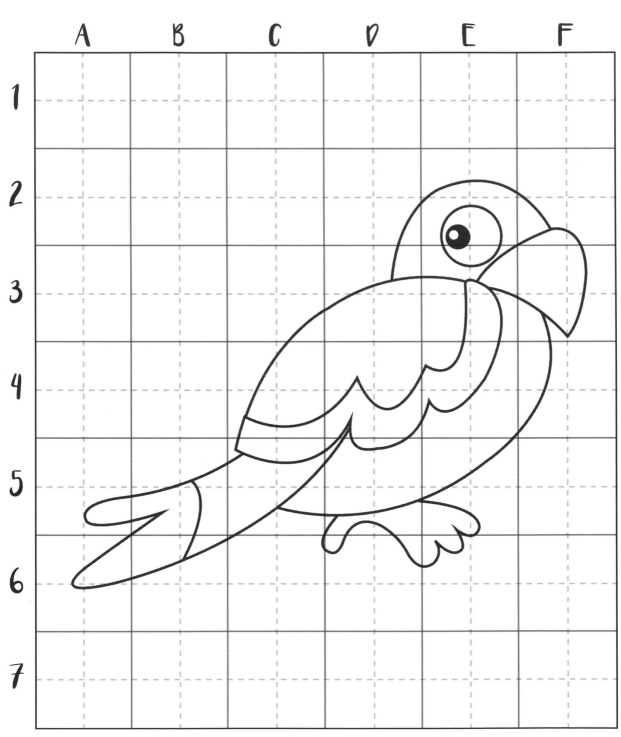

A B C D E F

1 2 3 4 5 6 7

Your turn!

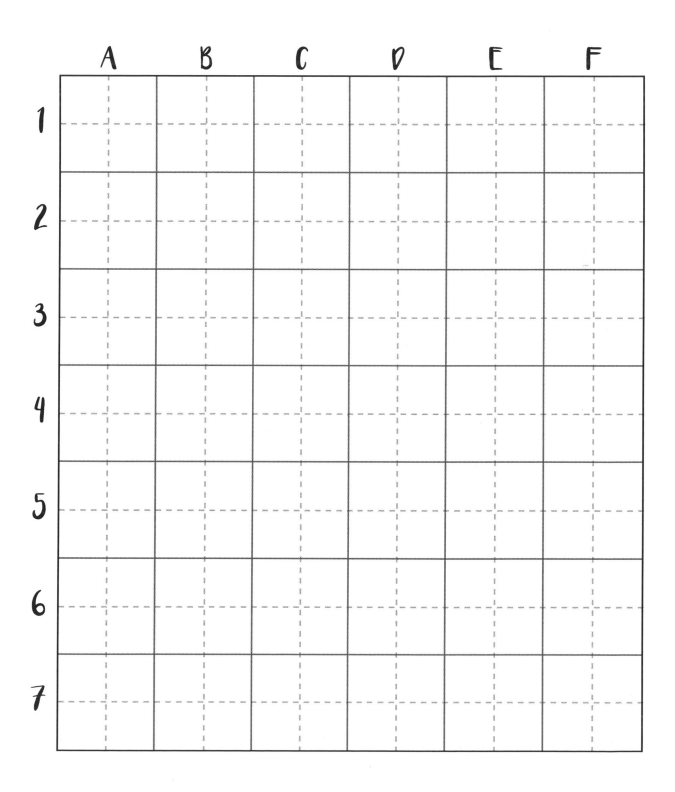

Trace it!

Try it on your own!

Tiger

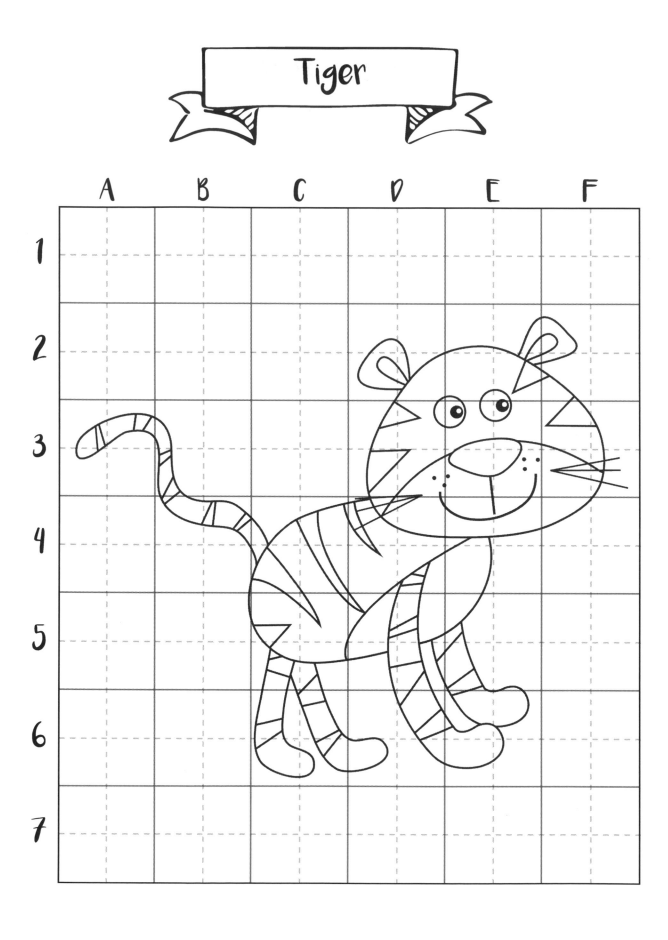

Your turn!

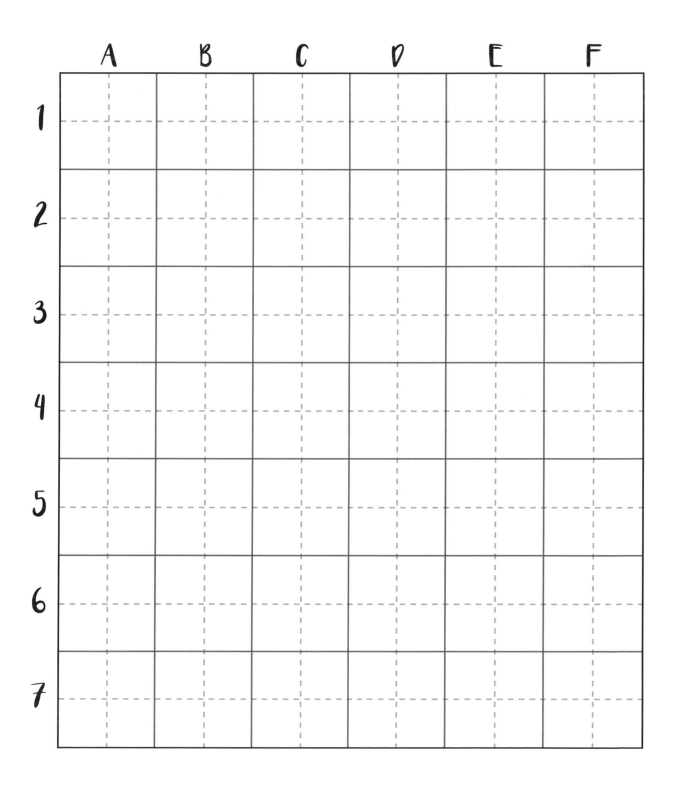

Trace it!

Try it on your own!

Zebra

A   B   C   D   E   F

1

2

3

4

5

6

7

Your turn!

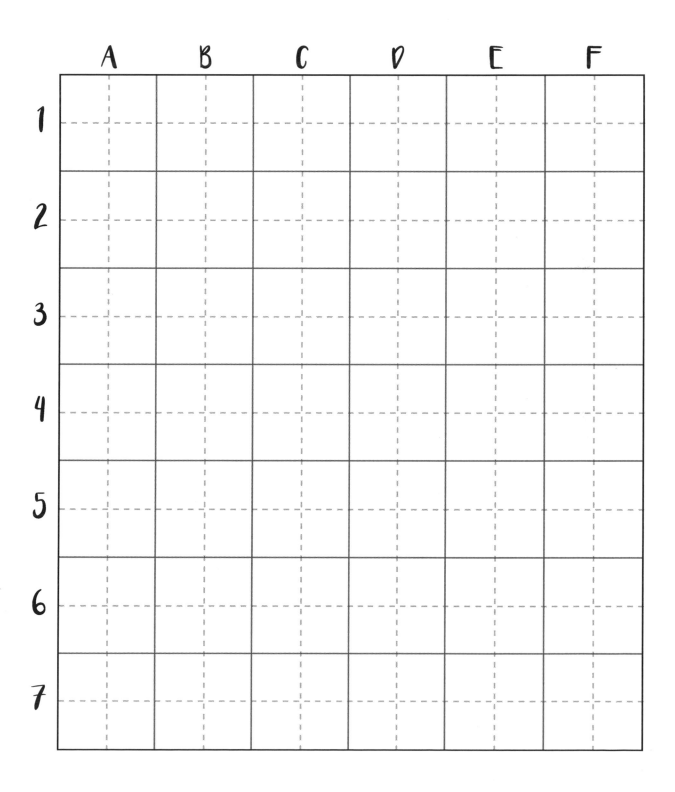

Trace it!

Try it on your own!

Snake

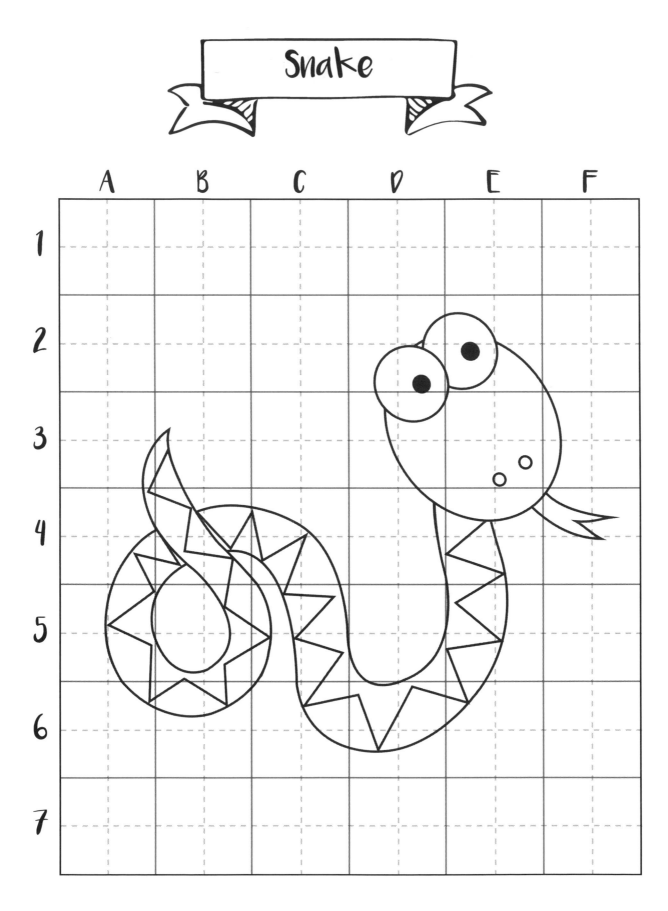

	A	B	C	D	E	F
1						
2						
3						
4						
5						
6						
7						

Your turn!

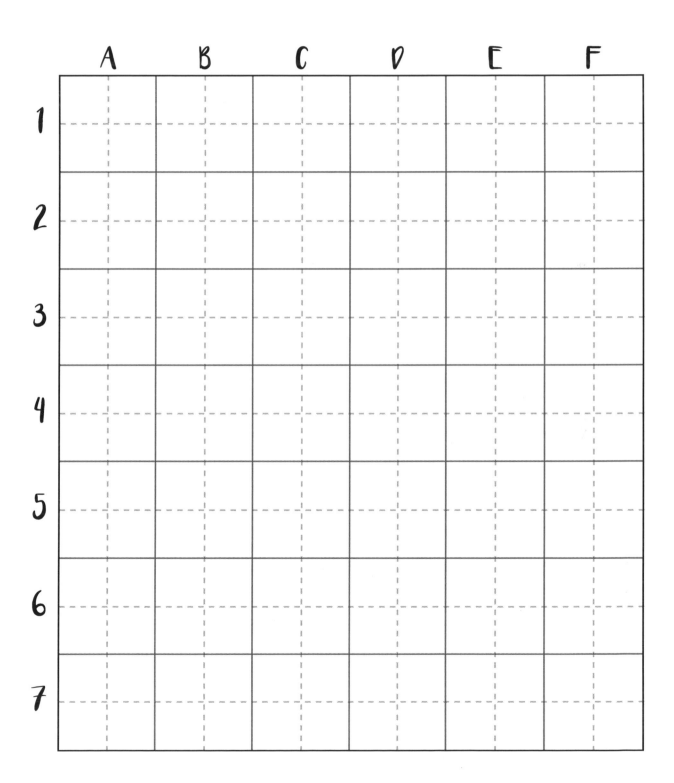

Trace it!

Try it on your own!

Bee

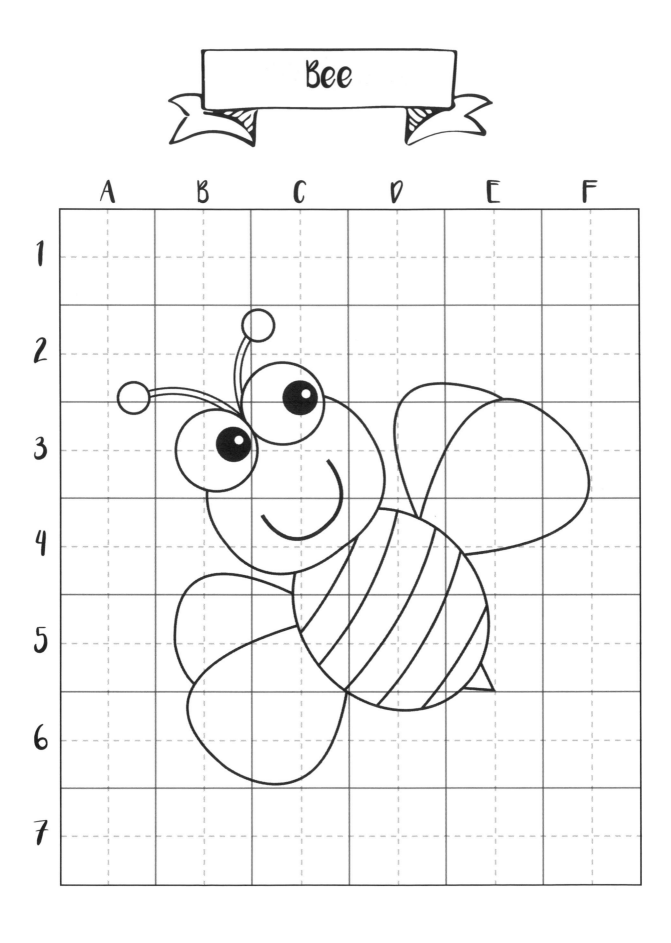

A B C D E F

1 2 3 4 5 6 7

Your turn!

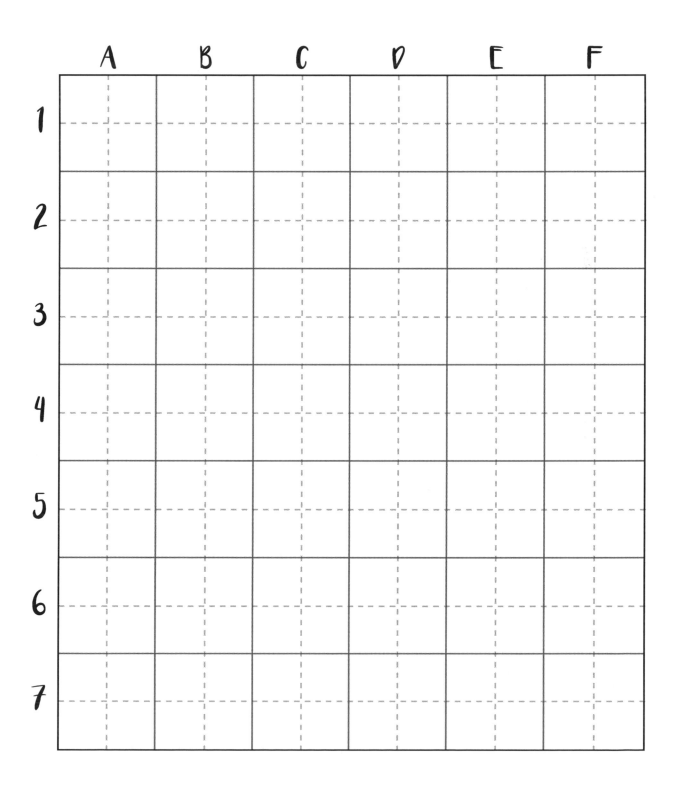

Trace it!

Try it on your own!

practice, practice, practice!

way to go!

lookin' good!

keep it up!